Pet's Photo

MW01537165

Breed _____

D.O.B _____

Sex _____

ID's Chip _____

Rabies Tag _____

Neutered/Spayed _____

Color/Markings _____

VET _____ Phone _____

Groomed _____ Phone _____

PET INFORMATION

Medications and Allergies

_____
_____
_____

Favorite Foods

_____
_____

Favorite Activities

_____
_____

CLUB REGISTRATION AND MEMBERSHIPS

Club's Name _____

Registration Name _____

Registration Number _____

HEALTH RECORD

Date	Physical Test	Fecal Test	Wormer Given	Heartworms Test	Surgery

PET VACCINATIONS

Date	Vaccine	Exp. Date	Certificate

PET IMMUZATION RECORD

Date	Age	Type	Given by	Next Due

APPOINTMENT NOTES

Date: _____   Time: _____

VET: _____

Reason for visit: _____

_____

_____

Weight: _____ Next Appt.: _____

Notes & Concerns: _____

_____

_____

_____

_____

_____

Date: _____   Time: _____

VET: _____

Reason for visit: _____

_____

_____

Weight: _____ Next Appt.: _____

Notes & Concerns: _____

_____

_____

_____

_____

PET EXPENSE LOG

DATE	CATEGORY				COST
	Food	VET	Meds	Grooming	
					$
					$
					$
					$
					$
					$
					$
					$
					$
					$
					$
					$
					$
					$
					$
					$
					$
					$
					$
					$
					$
					$
					$
					$
					$

MY FURBABY JOURNAL

MY FURBABY JOURNAL

MY FURBABY JOURNAL

_____
_____
_____
_____
_____
_____
_____
_____
_____
_____
_____
_____
_____
_____
_____
_____
_____
_____
_____
_____
_____
_____
_____
_____

MY FURBABY JOURNAL

photos

HEALTH RECORD

Date	Physical Test	Fecal Test	Wormer Given	Heartworms Test	Surgery

PET VACCINATIONS

Date	Vaccine	Exp. Date	Certificate

PET IMMUZATION RECORD

Date	Age	Type	Given by	Next Due

APPOINTMENT NOTES

Date: _____   Time: _____

VET: _____

Reason for visit: _____

_____

_____

Weight: _____ Next Appt.: _____

Notes & Concerns: _____

_____

_____

_____

_____

_____

Date: _____   Time: _____

VET: _____

Reason for visit: _____

_____

_____

Weight: _____ Next Appt.: _____

Notes & Concerns: _____

_____

_____

_____

_____

PET EXPENSE LOG

DATE	CATEGORY				COST
	Food	VET	Meds	Grooming	
					$
					$
					$
					$
					$
					$
					$
					$
					$
					$
					$
					$
					$
					$
					$
					$
					$
					$
					$
					$
					$
					$
					$
					$
					$
					$
					$

MY FURBABY JOURNAL

MY FURBABY JOURNAL

MY FURBABY JOURNAL

MY FURBABY JOURNAL

photos

HEALTH RECORD

Date	Physical Test	Fecal Test	Wormer Given	Heartworms Test	Surgery

PET VACCINATIONS

Date	Vaccine	Exp. Date	Certificate

PET IMMUZATION RECORD

Date	Age	Type	Given by	Next Due

APPOINTMENT NOTES

Date: _____   Time: _____

VET: _____

Reason for visit: _____

_____

_____

Weight: _____ Next Appt.: _____

Notes & Concerns: _____

_____

_____

_____

_____

_____

Date: _____   Time: _____

VET: _____

Reason for visit: _____

_____

_____

Weight: _____ Next Appt.: _____

Notes & Concerns: _____

_____

_____

_____

_____

_____

PET EXPENSE LOG

DATE	CATEGORY				COST
	Food	VET	Meds	Grooming	
					$
					$
					$
					$
					$
					$
					$
					$
					$
					$
					$
					$
					$
					$
					$
					$
					$
					$
					$
					$
					$
					$
					$
					$
					$
					$
					$

MY FURBABY JOURNAL

MY FURBABY JOURNAL

MY FURBABY JOURNAL

MY FURBABY JOURNAL

photos

HEALTH RECORD

Date	Physical Test	Fecal Test	Wormer Given	Heartworms Test	Surgery

PET VACCINATIONS

Date	Vaccine	Exp. Date	Certificate

PET IMMUZATION RECORD

Date	Age	Type	Given by	Next Due

APPOINTMENT NOTES

Date: _____ Time: _____

VET: _____

Reason for visit: _____

_____

_____

Weight: _____ Next Appt.: _____

Notes & Concerns: _____

_____

_____

_____

_____

_____

Date: _____ Time: _____

VET: _____

Reason for visit: _____

_____

_____

Weight: _____ Next Appt.: _____

Notes & Concerns: _____

_____

_____

_____

_____

PET EXPENSE LOG

DATE	CATEGORY				COST
	Food	VET	Meds	Grooming	
					$
					$
					$
					$
					$
					$
					$
					$
					$
					$
					$
					$
					$
					$
					$
					$
					$
					$
					$
					$
					$
					$
					$
					$
					$

MY FURBABY JOURNAL

MY FURBABY JOURNAL

MY FURBABY JOURNAL

MY FURBABY JOURNAL

photos

HEALTH RECORD

Date	Physical Test	Fecal Test	Wormer Given	Heartworms Test	Surgery

PET VACCINATIONS

Date	Vaccine	Exp. Date	Certificate

PET IMMUZATION RECORD

Date	Age	Type	Given by	Next Due

APPOINTMENT NOTES

Date: _____   Time: _____

VET: _____

Reason for visit: _____

_____

_____

Weight: _____ Next Appt.: _____

Notes & Concerns: _____

_____

_____

_____

_____

_____

Date: _____   Time: _____

VET: _____

Reason for visit: _____

_____

_____

Weight: _____ Next Appt.: _____

Notes & Concerns: _____

_____

_____

_____

_____

PET EXPENSE LOG

DATE	CATEGORY				COST
	Food	VET	Meds	Grooming	
					$
					$
					$
					$
					$
					$
					$
					$
					$
					$
					$
					$
					$
					$
					$
					$
					$
					$
					$
					$
					$
					$
					$
					$
					$
					$
					$

MY FURBABY JOURNAL

MY FURBABY JOURNAL

MY FURBABY JOURNAL

MY FURBABY JOURNAL

photos

HEALTH RECORD

Date	Physical Test	Fecal Test	Wormer Given	Heartworms Test	Surgery

PET VACCINATIONS

Date	Vaccine	Exp. Date	Certificate

PET IMMUZATION RECORD

Date	Age	Type	Given by	Next Due

APPOINTMENT NOTES

Date: _____   Time: _____

VET: _____

Reason for visit: _____

_____

_____

Weight: _____   Next Appt.: _____

Notes & Concerns: _____

_____

_____

_____

_____

_____

Date: _____   Time: _____

VET: _____

Reason for visit: _____

_____

_____

Weight: _____   Next Appt.: _____

Notes & Concerns: _____

_____

_____

_____

_____

PET EXPENSE LOG

DATE	CATEGORY				COST
	Food	VET	Meds	Grooming	
					$
					$
					$
					$
					$
					$
					$
					$
					$
					$
					$
					$
					$
					$
					$
					$
					$
					$
					$
					$
					$
					$
					$
					$
					$
					$

MY FURBABY JOURNAL

MY FURBABY JOURNAL

MY FURBABY JOURNAL

MY FURBABY JOURNAL

photos

HEALTH RECORD

Date	Physical Test	Fecal Test	Wormer Given	Heartworms Test	Surgery

PET VACCINATIONS

Date	Vaccine	Exp. Date	Certificate

PET IMMUZATION RECORD

Date	Age	Type	Given by	Next Due

APPOINTMENT NOTES

Date: _____   Time: _____

VET: _____

Reason for visit: _____

_____

_____

Weight: _____   Next Appt.: _____

Notes & Concerns: _____

_____

_____

_____

_____

_____

Date: _____   Time: _____

VET: _____

Reason for visit: _____

_____

_____

Weight: _____   Next Appt.: _____

Notes & Concerns: _____

_____

_____

_____

_____

PET EXPENSE LOG

DATE	CATEGORY				COST
	Food	VET	Meds	Grooming	
					$
					$
					$
					$
					$
					$
					$
					$
					$
					$
					$
					$
					$
					$
					$
					$
					$
					$
					$
					$
					$
					$
					$
					$
					$

MY FURBABY JOURNAL

MY FURBABY JOURNAL

MY FURBABY JOURNAL

MY FURBABY JOURNAL

photos

HEALTH RECORD

Date	Physical Test	Fecal Test	Wormer Given	Heartworms Test	Surgery

PET VACCINATIONS

Date	Vaccine	Exp. Date	Certificate

PET IMMUZATION RECORD

Date	Age	Type	Given by	Next Due

APPOINTMENT NOTES

Date: _____   Time: _____

VET: _____

Reason for visit: _____

_____

_____

Weight: _____ Next Appt.: _____

Notes & Concerns: _____

_____

_____

_____

_____

_____

Date: _____   Time: _____

VET: _____

Reason for visit: _____

_____

_____

Weight: _____ Next Appt.: _____

Notes & Concerns: _____

_____

_____

_____

_____

PET EXPENSE LOG

DATE	CATEGORY				COST
	Food	VET	Meds	Grooming	
					$
					$
					$
					$
					$
					$
					$
					$
					$
					$
					$
					$
					$
					$
					$
					$
					$
					$
					$
					$
					$
					$
					$
					$
					$
					$

MY FURBABY JOURNAL

MY FURBABY JOURNAL

MY FURBABY JOURNAL

MY FURBABY JOURNAL

photos

HEALTH RECORD

Date	Physical Test	Fecal Test	Wormer Given	Heartworms Test	Surgery

PET VACCINATIONS

Date	Vaccine	Exp. Date	Certificate

PET IMMUZATION RECORD

Date	Age	Type	Given by	Next Due

APPOINTMENT NOTES

Date: _____   Time: _____

VET: _____

Reason for visit: _____

_____

_____

Weight: _____ Next Appt.: _____

Notes & Concerns: _____

_____

_____

_____

_____

_____

Date: _____   Time: _____

VET: _____

Reason for visit: _____

_____

_____

Weight: _____ Next Appt.: _____

Notes & Concerns: _____

_____

_____

_____

_____

PET EXPENSE LOG

DATE	CATEGORY				COST
	Food	VET	Meds	Grooming	
					$
					$
					$
					$
					$
					$
					$
					$
					$
					$
					$
					$
					$
					$
					$
					$
					$
					$
					$
					$
					$
					$
					$
					$

MY FURBABY JOURNAL

MY FURBABY JOURNAL

MY FURBABY JOURNAL

MY FURBABY JOURNAL

photos

HEALTH RECORD

Date	Physical Test	Fecal Test	Wormer Given	Heartworms Test	Surgery

PET VACCINATIONS

Date	Vaccine	Exp. Date	Certificate

PET IMMUZATION RECORD

Date	Age	Type	Given by	Next Due

APPOINTMENT NOTES

Date: _____   Time: _____

VET: _____

Reason for visit: _____

_____

_____

Weight: _____ Next Appt.: _____

Notes & Concerns: _____

_____

_____

_____

_____

_____

Date: _____   Time: _____

VET: _____

Reason for visit: _____

_____

_____

Weight: _____ Next Appt.: _____

Notes & Concerns: _____

_____

_____

_____

_____

PET EXPENSE LOG

DATE	CATEGORY				COST
	Food	VET	Meds	Grooming	
					$
					$
					$
					$
					$
					$
					$
					$
					$
					$
					$
					$
					$
					$
					$
					$
					$
					$
					$
					$
					$
					$
					$
					$
					$

MY FURBABY JOURNAL

MY FURBABY JOURNAL

MY FURBABY JOURNAL

MY FURBABY JOURNAL

photos

HEALTH RECORD

Date	Physical Test	Fecal Test	Wormer Given	Heartworms Test	Surgery

PET VACCINATIONS

Date	Vaccine	Exp. Date	Certificate

PET IMMUZATION RECORD

Date	Age	Type	Given by	Next Due

APPOINTMENT NOTES

Date: _____   Time: _____

VET: _____

Reason for visit: _____

_____

_____

Weight: _____   Next Appt.: _____

Notes & Concerns: _____

_____

_____

_____

_____

_____

Date: _____   Time: _____

VET: _____

Reason for visit: _____

_____

_____

Weight: _____   Next Appt.: _____

Notes & Concerns: _____

_____

_____

_____

_____

PET EXPENSE LOG

DATE	CATEGORY				COST
	Food	VET	Meds	Grooming	
					$
					$
					$
					$
					$
					$
					$
					$
					$
					$
					$
					$
					$
					$
					$
					$
					$
					$
					$
					$
					$
					$
					$
					$
					$

MY FURBABY JOURNAL

MY FURBABY JOURNAL

MY FURBABY JOURNAL

MY FURBABY JOURNAL

photos

HEALTH RECORD

Date	Physical Test	Fecal Test	Wormer Given	Heartworms Test	Surgery

PET VACCINATIONS

Date	Vaccine	Exp. Date	Certificate

PET IMMUZATION RECORD

Date	Age	Type	Given by	Next Due

APPOINTMENT NOTES

Date: _____   Time: _____

VET: _____

Reason for visit: _____

_____

_____

Weight: _____ Next Appt.: _____

Notes & Concerns: _____

_____

_____

_____

_____

_____

_____

Date: _____   Time: _____

VET: _____

Reason for visit: _____

_____

_____

Weight: _____ Next Appt.: _____

Notes & Concerns: _____

_____

_____

_____

_____

PET EXPENSE LOG

DATE	CATEGORY				COST
	Food	VET	Meds	Grooming	
					$
					$
					$
					$
					$
					$
					$
					$
					$
					$
					$
					$
					$
					$
					$
					$
					$
					$
					$
					$
					$
					$
					$
					$
					$

MY FURBABY JOURNAL

MY FURBABY JOURNAL

MY FURBABY JOURNAL

MY FURBABY JOURNAL

photos